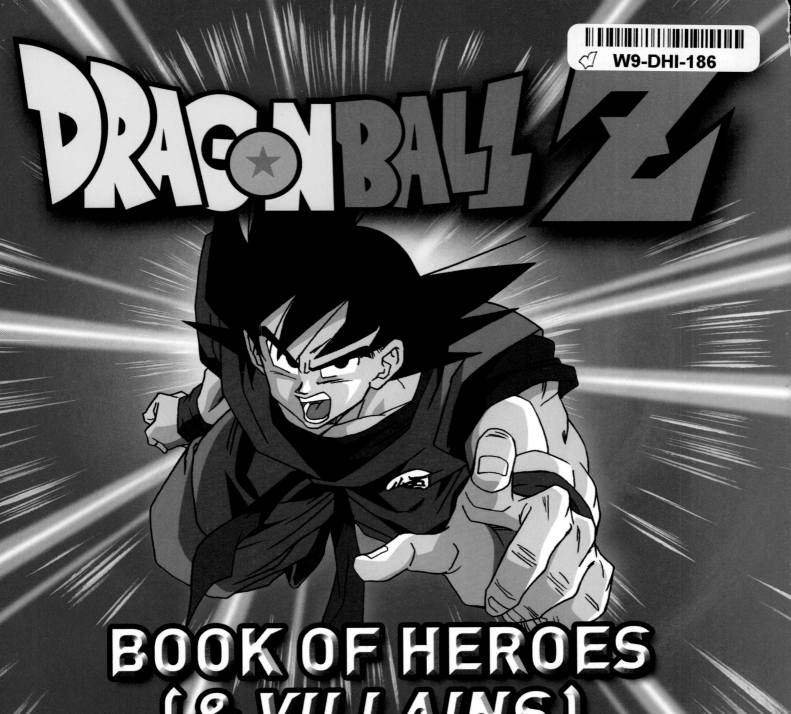

DRAGONBALL Z

BOOK OF HEROES (& VILLAINS)

By Jeff O'Hare

Scholastic Inc.

New York   Toronto   London   Auckland   Sydney
Mexico City   New Delhi   Hong Kong   Buenos Aires

Dragon Ball Z Code Wheel

ISBN 0-439-80172-9

© 2005 Bird Studio/Shueisha, TOEI ANIMATION. Licensed by FUNimation Productions, Ltd. All rights reserved. Dragon Ball Z® and all logos, character names and distinctive likenesses thereof are trademarks of TOEI ANIMATION.

Published by Scholastic Inc.

12 11 10 9 8 7 6 5 4 3 2 1   5 6 7 8 9/0

Designed by Kay Petronio

Printed in the U.S.A.

First printing, September 2005

ドラゴンボールZ

Are you ready to test your might and merit against the greatest warriors in the Dragon Ball Z universe? How do you match up with heroes like Goku and Vegeta, or against villains like Raditz and Frieza?

- Even if you think you know everything about Dragon Ball Z, you're sure to find new and exciting puzzles and questions on these pages. Amazing wishes, titanic battles, shifting shapes, horrifying creatures, and loyal friends are just part of the excitement. Prepare yourself, both mentally and physically, for the greatest challenges in the world of Dragon Ball Z!

- Some puzzles will refer to the **Dragon Ball Z Code Wheel** that can be found on the opposite page.

- Information about all the Dragon Ball Z heroes and villains has been encrypted into **secret codes** throughout this book. To decipher these messages, you will need to use the Dragon Ball Z Code Wheel.

- Beside each message will be a **symbol**. Look for that symbol on the Code Wheel. Beside the symbol is a **number**. This number is the position for the letter A when using that particular code. The **arrow** beside the number tells you whether to be counting up or down from that number in order to find the rest of the letters.

- For example, the **CLOUD** code is listed as 7〉. That means A is 7 and that you count up for the rest of the letters (7=A, 8=B, 9=C, and so on).

- The **STAR** code is listed as 35〈. That means A is 35 and that you count down from there for the rest of the letters (35=A, 34=B, 33=C, and so on).

- Every code is different, so you may need to chart out all the letters to decipher these messages.

- Once you become a master of the Dragon Ball Z Code Wheel, use it to send secret messages to your other Dragon Ball Z friends.

Unscramble these letters to find the name
of the planet where Goku was born:

GEEVAT

—— —— —— —— —— ——

Goku is related to each of the characters listed
here. Use the **SUN** code to decipher the names
and then describe how he or she is related to Goku.

_____
7-15-8-1-14

Relation: _____

_____
7-15-20-5-14

Relation: _____

_____
18-1-4-9-20-26

Relation: _____

_____
3-8-9 — 3-8-9

Relation: _____

_____
15-24 — 11-9-14-7

Relation: _____

Circle the name that Goku was given at birth:

A) Piccolo

B) Saiyan

C) Kakarot

4

In one version of the future, Goku dies from a disease.

The name of this disease can be found in the grid below. Start at the *H* and move from letter to letter in one continuous line until you use all the letters. You may move across, up, down, or diagonally. Your line may cross itself and one letter will be used twice.

```
H U S
E R I
A T V
```

H U S E R
H A T V B

WHO AM I?

I came from the future to warn Goku about his disease.

Decipher this list to find some of Goku's most impressive weapons and attacks.

_____
25-22-15-24-15-26   8-21-19-8

_____
17-7-19-11-14-7-19-11-14-7   29-7-28-11

_____
22-21-29-11-24   22-21-18-11

_____
17-7-15-21—17-7-15   7-26-26-7-9-17

_____.
15-20-25-26-7-20-26 26-24-7-20-25-19-15-25-25-15-21-20.

GOKU

5

Decipher this message to find Vegeta's goal in life.

_____

50-45   32-35   50-38-35   37-48-35-31-50-35-49-50

_____

49-31-39-55-31-44   31-42-39-52-35,   42-39-41-35   39

_____.

31-42-53-31-55-49   38-31-52-35   32-35-35-44.

Unscramble these letters to reveal the name of Vegeta's partner who came to Earth with him:

PAPAN

__ __ __ __ __

Match each planet to its relationship to Vegeta.

PLANET	SIGNIFICANCE
1. ARLIA	a. Home planet
2. EARTH	b. Visited this planet in search of immortality
3. NAMEK	c. Came to conquer this planet, then fought in its defense
4. VEGETA	d. Conquered and destroyed this planet

How does Vegeta fit into the ruling family of his home planet? _____

6

Circle the highest level of warrior that Vegeta has achieved:

A) Saiyan
B) Super Saiyan
C) Ascended Saiyan
D) Super Saiyan 3
E) Prime Saiyan

During a battle with Goku, Vegeta did something in order to turn into an Oozaru. To find out what he did, put in the letters found at the coordinates below each line. The first number will always be for the side going top to bottom, the second number will always be for the line across.

	1	2	3	4	5
1	A	C	D	E	H
2	M	N	O	R	T

___ ___   ___ ___ ___ ___ ___ ___ ___
1,5 1,4   1,2 2,4 1,4 1,1 2,5 1,4 1,3

___   ___ ___ ___ ___.
1,1   2,1 2,3 2,3 2,2

WHO AM I?

I cut off Vegeta's tail while he was in Oozaru form.

VEGETA

7

Draw a line between the coordinates given in each pair in order to spell out the name of the one pet that Buu loves.

```
    A   B   C   D   E   F

1   •   •   •   •   •   •

2   •   •   •   •   •   •

3   •   •   •   •   •   •
```

A1-A3, B1-B3, C1-C3, E1-E3, A3-B3, C3-D3, E3-F3, A1-B1, C1-D1, E1-F1, A2-B2, C2-D2, E2-F2

Unscramble these letters to reveal which character Evil Buu absorbs to become Super Buu:

UNIJA BUM

__ __ __ __   __ __ __

Identify each of these Buu incarnations with the right title, and then put them in order as they appeared in the Buu Cycle, from first to last.

Evil___   **Kid___**   **Super___**   **Majin___**

What character emerges that is actually all that is good in Buu?

_____

Who released Buu from his cocoon?
Circle the correct response.

A) Bibidi

B) Babidi

C) Kibito

WHO AM I?

I am the evil wizard
who first conjured up Buu.

When Buu was on a rampage to destroy Earth, one
fighter stepped forward to calm him. To find the
name of this person, choose only one letter from
each column.

F A R A I L E

G E S B O M I

H I T C U H O

_ _ _ _ _ _ _

This message will reveal why Raditz first came to Earth.

26-21   18-11-7-24-20

29-14-31   13-21-17-27

14-7-10-20-26

9-21-20-23-27-11-24-11-10

.

26-14-11   11-7-24-26-14.

At what level did Raditz come to Earth? Circle the correct response.

A) Saiyan
B) Super Saiyan
C) Ascended Saiyan

Unscramble these letters to find the name of the eyepiece Raditz wears:

DB2

COURTES

___ ___ ___ ___ ___ ___ ___

Decipher this list to find three of the powers of Raditz's eyepiece.

94-92-79-96-82   89-86-98-100-81-92-86-87

_____ ;

86-95   86-85-85-86-87-96-87-81-82

_____

100-98-81-82   100-82

_____ ;

98-86-88-88-80-87-92-98-100-81-86-83

_____

94-92-79-96-82   85-86-78-96-83

_____

89-96-79-96-89 86-95 86-85-85-86-87-96-87-81-82

WHO AM I?

Who sacrificed himself to ensure the end of Raditz?

_____

I sacrificed myself to rid the world of Nappa.

11

raditz ™

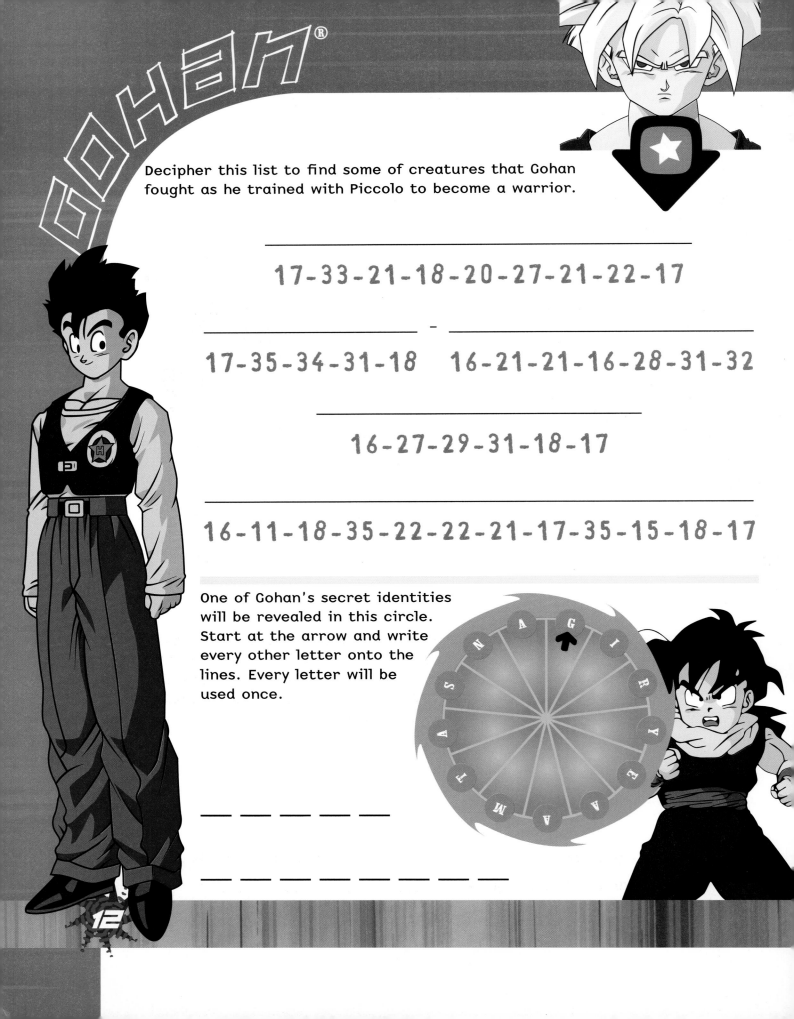

GOHAN®

Decipher this list to find some of creatures that Gohan fought as he trained with Piccolo to become a warrior.

_____
17-33-21-18-20-27-21-22-17

-

_____   _____
17-35-34-31-18   16-21-21-16-28-31-32

_____
16-27-29-31-18-17

_____
16-11-18-35-22-22-21-17-35-15-18-17

One of Gohan's secret identities will be revealed in this circle. Start at the arrow and write every other letter onto the lines. Every letter will be used once.

_ _ _ _ _

_ _ _ _ _ _ _ _

Who heals Gohan after he is injured battling Buu? Circle the correct response.

A) Supreme Kai
B) Kibito
C) Dabura

Gohan meets his future wife while they are in high school together. Unscramble these letters to reveal her name:

LIVED

_ _ _ _ _

Now unscramble these letters to reveal the name of her father, a great fighter in his own right:

LURCHEE

_ _ _ _ _ _ _

WHO AM I?

I can change my enemies to stone by spitting on them.

One of Gohan's mighty feats of strength was to retrieve a sword for the Supreme Kai. The name of that object is hidden in this grid. Start at the L and move from letter to letter in one continuous line until you use all the letters. You may move across, up, down, or diagonally. Your line may cross itself, and some letters may be used more than once.

```
L Z R
E Y A
G N D
```
_ _ _ _ _ _ _ _ _ _ _ _ Sword

DB3

Decipher this message to reveal the name of a creature that Gohan can transform into. _____

35-35-46-21-38-41

GOHAN

13

The names of the first two villains defeated by Trunks when he arrived back in time are scrambled together here. Unscramble the following phrase to find the two evil names.

BYROAD FICKLE
ZINC ROGG

_ _ _ _ _ _ _ _ _

and _ _ _ _ _ _ _ _

Circle the character Trunks and Goten can fuse together to form.

A) Gotenks

B) Gohan

C) Imperfect Cell

In order for this fusion to take place, what must Trunks do with his power? _____

Decipher this message to find where Trunks came from when he first appears in Dragon Ball Z.

3   13-43-41-43-37-11

7-31-29-41-37-31-25-25-11-9

5-51   3-29-9-37-31-19-9-39

The names of Trunks's parents can be found in this grid. Start at the *V* and move from letter to letter in one continuous line until you find the first name. Then start at the *B* to draw a line through the other name. You may move across, up, down, or diagonally. Your line may cross itself, and some letters may be used more than once.

A M L
G T U
V E B

___ ___ ___ ___ ___ ___ and

___ ___ ___ ___ ___

I trained Trunks while we were in the Hyperbolic Time Chamber.

Without using any names that start with G-O, name two characters that Goten is related to: _____ and _____.

Solve this equation to find out how old Goten was when he entered his first tournament:

Take the number of quadrants ruled by the Kais and add that number to the number of levels in Babidi's spaceship.

_____

Goten teamed up with Trunks in a new identity to battle Android 18. That identity is hidden in this grid. Start at the M and move from letter to letter in one continuous line until you use all the letters. You may move across, up, down, or diagonally. Your line may cross itself, and some letters may be used more than once.

```
S K T
A Y H
M I G
```

_ _ _ _ _ _   _ _ _

Decipher this list to learn some facts about Goten.

DB4

_____

57-54   52-50-63   55-61-74

16

57-54   52-50-63
_____

69-70-67-63
_____

68-70-65-54-67
_____

68-50-58-74-50-63
_____

72-58-69-57-64-70-69
_____

69-67-50-58-63-58-63-56   57-54   58-68
_____.

65-70-67-54   64-55   57-54-50-67-69.

Draw a line between the coordinates given in each pair in order to find the number of minutes that Goten and Trunks can stay fused.

	A	B	C	D
1	*	*	*	*
2	*	*	*	*
3	*	*	*	*

D1-D2, C1-C2, B1-B2, C3-D3, A3-B3, B2-B3,
C2-C3, D2-D3, D1-C1, B1-A1, B2-A2

Decipher this message to reveal the prize offered in Goten's first Junior Division Battle:

_____

1 12-5-19-19-15-14   6-18-15-13   8-5-18-3-21-12-5

Which Android was really Dr. Gero in disguise?
Circle the correct response.

A) 16

B) 18

C) 20

To find the location of Dr. Gero's hidden laboratory, write in the letters using the coordinates to the grid below. The first number will always be for the side going top to bottom, the second number will always be for the row across.

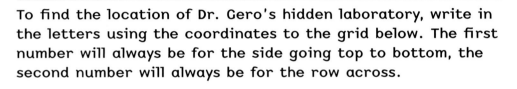

	1	2	3	4
1	A	B	C	D
2	E	H	I	N
3	O	R	S	T
4	U	V	W	Y

___ ___   ___   ___ ___ ___ ___
2,3 2,4   1,1   1,3 1,1 4,2 2,1

___ ___ ___ ___ ___ ___ ___
3,1 4,1 3,4 3,3 2,3 1,4 2,1

___ ___ ___ ___ ___   ___ ___ ___ ___.
2,4 3,1 3,2 3,4 2,2   1,3 2,3 3,4 4,4

Decipher this message to reveal the tool that allowed Dr. Gero to control his android creations.

73-65-73-60-71-73-64-75-53

59-57-59-62-73-64-59-69-63-64

75-63-64-58-60-63-66-66-73-60

Which of these androids did Dr. Gero not want activated?
Circle the correct response.

A) 16

B) 17

C) 18

WHO AM I?

I am the bodyguard for the Supreme Kai.

Unscramble these letters to find the first of the Dragon Ball Z fighters who was defeated by the Androids:

MACHAY

___ ___ ___ ___ ___ ___

Match each Android to an ability:

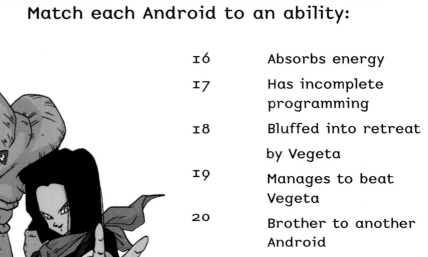

16	Absorbs energy
17	Has incomplete programming
18	Bluffed into retreat by Vegeta
19	Manages to beat Vegeta
20	Brother to another Android

Who convinced Android 18 to forfeit the World Martial Arts Tournament? Circle the correct response.

A) Krillin

B) Vegeta

C) Hercule

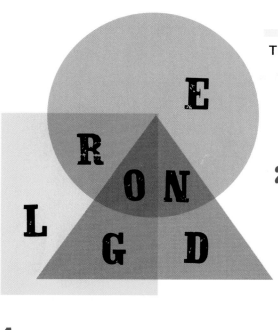

The name of the inventor of the Androids can be found by following the directions.

1. The first letter is in the triangle only: _____

2. The second letter is in the square and the circle, but not the triangle: _____

3. The third letter is in the triangle and the square, but not the circle: _____

4. The fourth letter is in the circle only: _____

5. The fifth letter is the same as the second letter: _____

6. The sixth letter is shared by all three shapes: _____

___ ___ ___ ___ ___ ___

The evil villain Cell set out to absorb which two androids? _____ and _____.

WHO AM I?

I guard the first level of Babidi's spaceship.

CELL

Match each name to one of Cell's forms.

Imperfect   Perfect   Junior

What does Cell have in common with Androids 17 and 18?

_____

DB6

Decipher this code to make a list of the names of some of the characters whose DNA helped to create Cell.

_____
81-74-68-68-80-77-80

_____
87-70-72-70-85-66

_____
71-83-74-70-91-66

_____
72-80-76-86

One of the benefits of Cell's scorpion tail can be found in this grid. Start at the A and move from letter to letter in one continuous line until you use all the letters. You may move across, up, down, or diagonally. Your line may cross itself, and some letters may be used more than once.

```
G E N
Y R S          _ _ _ _ _ _ _ _
A B O          _ _ _ _ _ _
```

Which of these is not one of Cell's powers? Circle the correct response.

A) Regeneration
B) Cloning
C) Fire Breath

Unscramble these letters to find the name of the hero who finally defeated Cell:

HOGAN

— — — — —

Cell received a great power from Goku's DNA. To find the name of this technique, start at the arrow and then go around the circle clockwise, writing every fourth letter you come to on the lines. Every letter will be used once.

_ _ _ _ _ _ _

_ _ _ _ _ _ _ _ _ _

WHO AM I?

I have three eyes.

CELL

Circle King Kai in this group of Kais.

Match each of the four quadrants of the universe with what it is best known for.

1. North
2. East
3. South
4. West

a. Peaceful area of space
b. Home of great warriors
c. Earth is in this quadrant
d. Produces speedy fighters

Put these Kais in order, beginning with the top ruler.

King Kai   1._____

Supreme Kai   2._____

Grand Kai   3._____

Decipher this message to find the names of King Kai's two companions.

_____

14-36-10-14-30-36-50   40-16-10

_____

14-36-2-38-38-16-30-32-32-10-36

_____

2-28-8   4-42-4-4-24-10-38

_____.

40-16-10   26-30-28-22-10-50.

To find the name of the original rulers of
the Kais, write in the letters found at the
coordinates below each line. The first number
will always be for the side going top to bottom,
the second number will always be for the
horizontal row of letters.

	1	2	3
1	A	D	H
2	I	K	O

__ __ __ __ __ __ __ __
1,2 1,1 2,1 2,2 1,1 2,1 2,3 1,3

WHO AM I?

I was the West Kai's greatest warrior.

KING KAI™

25

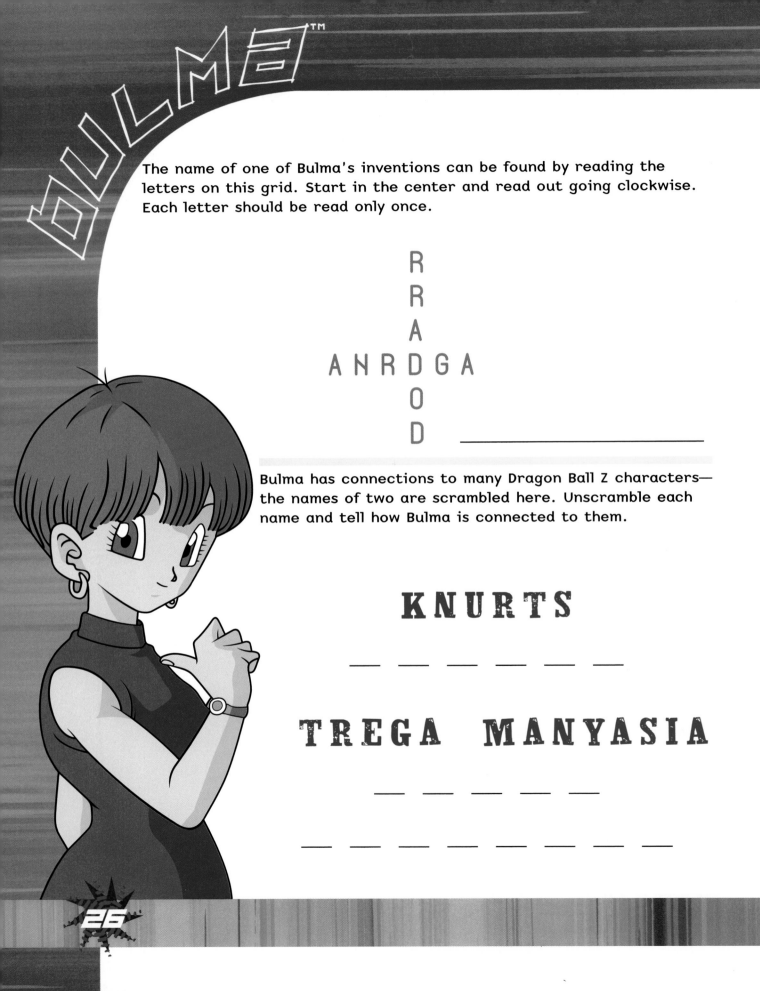

BULMA™

The name of one of Bulma's inventions can be found by reading the letters on this grid. Start in the center and read out going clockwise. Each letter should be read only once.

```
        R
        R
        A
A N R D G A
        O
        D
```
_____

Bulma has connections to many Dragon Ball Z characters—the names of two are scrambled here. Unscramble each name and tell how Bulma is connected to them.

KNURTS

_ _ _ _ _ _

TREGA MANYASIA

_ _ _ _ _   _ _ _ _ _ _ _

26

Decipher this list to find the names of two people who went into space with Bulma, along with the name of the planet they visited.

_____
25-18-27-24-24-27-22

_____
29-21-28-35-22

_____
22-35-23-31-25

Bulma is a technical genius who helped rebuild what character? _____

What is Bulma's most distinct personality trait? Circle the correct response below.

A) She snores.
B) She can't stop talking.
C) She sneezes when danger is around.

WHO AM I?

I am the Captain of an evil fighting force that bears my name.

Decipher this code to reveal some of Pan's personality traits.

DB1

29-42-49-33-50-37-31

32-35-30-37-40-26

45-46-50-33-39-46-32-32

Who are Pan's parents? Circle the correct response below.

A) Hercule and Videl
B) Goku and Chi-chi
C) Gohan and Videl
D) Krillan and Android 18

Find the path that will lead Pan to her favorite treat.

Decipher this message to find the name of Pan's first competition.

29-21-24-18-10   19-7-24-26-15-7-18

7-24-26-25

26-21-27-24-20-7-19-11-20-26

WHO AM I?

I created the Earth's Dragon Balls.

Decipher this code to find a list of some of Piccolo's most impressive weapons and attacks.

98-100-87   83-96-94-96-87-96-83-100-81-96

89-92-88-99-82

96-87-96-83-94-76   99-89-100-82-81-82

82-80-85-96-83   82-85-96-96-97

99-96-100-88   98-100-87-87-86-87

95-92-87-100-89   95-89-100-82-93

98-100-87   98-89-86-87-96

93-92-88-82-96-89-95

Unscramble these letters to find the level of fighter that Piccolo hoped to achieve by fusing with Kami:

MAKE PRUNES

———— ————

How did Piccolo come into being? The answer to this question is hidden in these letters. To find it, first follow the three directions. Then circle the remaining words.

```
G  R  K  N  A  M  E  K
Y  L  L  A  U  T  C  A
S  E  H  R  M  R  F  G
L  I  V  E  D  I  S  O
```

1. Every time you find it, cross out the first initial of the person who told Piccolo he was an alien on Earth.

2. Every time you find it, cross out the first initial of the person Piccolo trained in an alternate universe.

3. Cross out the name of Piccolo's home planet.

Now circle all the remaining words and arrange them to answer the question. (Hint: one word is the whole second row backwards. There will be one more backward word on the bottom row, and two words will run diagonally.)

—— ' —— ——————— ————

———— ———— ————.

Circle the character Piccolo merged with to battle Frieza:

A) Vegeta

B) Pan

C) Nail

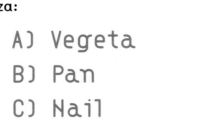

WHO AM I?

I am the living form of all of Majin Buu's anger.

Master Roshi is known by two other names. To find them, write in the letters found at the coordinates below each line. The first number will always be for the side going top to bottom, the second number will always be for the horizontal row of letters.

	1	2	3	4	5
1	A	E	H	I	L
2	M	R	S	T	U

— — — — — —   — — — — — —
2,4 2,5 2,2 2,4 1,5 1,2   1,3 1,2 2,2 2,1 1,4 2,4

— — — — — —   — — — — — —
1,3 1,2 2,2 2,1 1,4 2,4   2,4 2,5 2,2 2,4 1,5 1,2

How did Master Roshi get these nicknames? _____

Decipher this message to find one of Master Roshi's most important accomplishments.

26-29-38-39-40   25-21-38-40-28-32-29-34-27

40-35   34-41-38-40-41-38-25   21-34-24

23-35-34-40-38-35-32   40-28-25

36-35-43-25-38   35-26   32-29-27-28-40

Which pair of students studied under Master Roshi? Circle the correct pair below.

A) Goku & Krillin
B) Goku & Vegeta
C) Goten & Trunks
D) Gohan & Raditz

The name of an attack that Master Roshi taught both students can be found by following the directions below.

1. Letters two, six, ten, and twelve is shared by all three shapes.

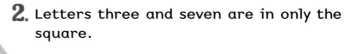

2. Letters three and seven are in only the square.

3. Letters four, eight, and fourteen are in the circle and the triangle.

4. Letter thirteen is in the circle only.

5. Letter eleven is in only the triangle and the square.

6. Letters five and nine are share by only the circle and square.

7. Letter one is in the triangle only.

— — — — — — — — — —   — — — —
I 2 3 4 5 6 7 8 9 10   11 12 13 14

WHO AM I?

I enjoy baseball and my mother wanted me to be a scholar.

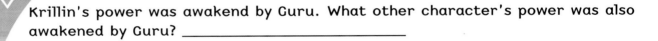

Krillin's power was awakend by Guru. What other character's power was also awakened by Guru? _____

Krillin studied with Goku to become a great fighter. The name of their teacher can be found in this grid. Start at the *M* and move from letter to letter in one continuous line until you use all the letters. You may move across, up, down, or diagonally. Your line may cross itself, and some letters will be used more than once.

```
H O R
I S E
M A T
```

— — — — — — — — — — — —

Decipher this list to find some interesting facts about Krillin.

_____

62-50-67-67-58-54-68   50-63

_____

50-63-53-67-64-58-53

_____

62-50-67-64-63   58-68   57-58-68

_____

53-50-70-56-57-69-54-67

_____

57-54-68   50-63   54-50-67-69-57-61-58-63-56

Unscramble these letters to find something important that Krillin shares with his fellow warriors:

ZANNUS BEES

_____ _____

What is Krillin's most powerful attack? Circle the correct response below.

A) Destructo Disk
B) Ginyu Kick
C) Recoome Kick

WHO AM I?

I was trapped in the Legendary Z Sword.

KRILLIN

Decipher this message to reveal Frieza's reputation.

_____

38-35-49   50-38-35   43-45-49-50

_____

46-45-53-35-48-36-51-42   31-44-34

_____

35-52-39-42   32-35-39-44-37   39-44

_____.

50-38-35   51-44-39-52-35-48-49-35.

The names of Frieza's two henchmen are fused together here. Separate them by writing down every other letter.

DZOADROBROINA

_ _ _ _ _ _ _ _ and _ _ _ _ _ _ _

Frieza used a group of fighters to hold the Dragon Balls on Namek. The name of this group can be found by reading the letters on this grid. Start in the center and read out going clockwise. Each letter should be read only once.

```
        O
    O N
  E F I G Y R        _ _ _ _ _
    U
    C                _ _ _ _ _
```

Decipher this list to reveal the five different forms Frieza uses during the Dragon Ball Z saga.

69-64   77   59-62-77-75-73   62-63-74

66-77-60-71-73   55-69-58-70   70-63-60-64-59

66-77-60-71-73-59-58   55-69-58-70

76-73-64-58   76-77-75-67

59-65-77-66-66-73-60   62-73-60-72-73-75-58

72-63-60-65

75-53-76-63-60-71

Who gave Frieza the material for his

cyborg form? _____

_____

WHO AM I?

I am Earth's dragon.

FRIEZA ®

DB5

37

GARLIC JR. ™

Which area is Garlic Jr.'s specialty? Circle the correct response below.

A) Physical powers
B) Mental powers
C) Healing powers

Unscramble these letters to reveal the name of the character who granted immortality to Garlic Jr.

NOSHNER

N O _ _ _ _ _

Decipher the code to reveal the names of the members of Garlic Jr.'s gang of henchmen.

78-86-84-85-66-83-69

84-81-74-68-70

84-66-77-85

87-74-79-70-72-66-83

85-73-70   84-81-74-68-70

67-80-90-84

Garlic Jr. came to Earth from somewhere in space. The name of that spot can be found in this circle. Start at the letter indicated by the arrow. Go around the circle in a clockwise manner writing down every third letter. All letters will be used once.

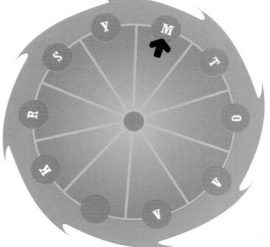

_ _ _ _ _ _ _ _ _

After becoming immortal, Garlic Jr. was banished from Earth. The name of the dimension where he was sent can be found in this grid. Start at the *D* and move from letter to letter in one continuous line until you use all the letters. You may move across, up, down, or diagonally. Your line may cross itself, and some letters may be used more than once.

O Z D   _ _ _ _

N E A   _ _ _ _

Only one thing can free a person from Garlic Jr.'s control. The name of this antidote can be found by reading the letters on this grid. Start in the center and read out going clockwise. Each letter should be read only once.

R
W
C
E D A S R A   _ _ _ _ _ _
E
T   _ _ _ _ _

WHO AM I?

I am the fusion form of Supreme Kai and Kibito.

Decipher this code to find a list of the three different wishes Dende helped to make on the Dragon Balls.

_____

4-36-18-28-14   32-18-6-6-30-24-30

_____

4-2-6-22   40-30   24-18-12-10

_____

36-10-40-42-36-28   14-30-22-42-38

_____

10-28-10-36-14-50

_____

4-36-18-28-14   10-2-36-40-16-24-18-28-14-38

_____

4-2-6-22   40-30   24-18-12-10

Who did Dende replace as guardian of planet Earth? Circle the correct response below.

A) Piccolo
B) Kami
C) Krillin

The names of the two people Dende lives with are fused together here.
Separate them by writing down every other letter.

PMIRCPCOOPLOO

__ __ __ __ __ __ __ and __ __. __ __ __ __ __

What is Dende's main power?

_____

Dende created a set of Dragon Balls. How many wishes do his Dragon
Balls grant? _____

WHO AM I?

I am the fusion form of Goku and Vegeta.

dende™

41

SAIYANS™

Decipher this list of characters who have achieved the level of Super Saiyan, then match with an image on the next page.

_____
15-31-23-43

_____
15-31-17-3-29

_____
15-31-41-11-29

_____
45-11-15-11-41-3

_____
41-37-43-29-23-39

_____
15-31-41-11-29-23-39

Which of these characters never received a Saiyan ranking? Circle the correct response below.

A) Raditz
B) Piccolo
C) Nappa

WHO AM I?

I existed in one universe as both a baby and a teenager at the same time.

ANSWERS

PAGES 4–5 — GOKU®

Unscramble these letters: VEGETA

Gohan is Goku's oldest son.
Goten is Goku's youngest son.
Raditz is his brother.
Chi-chi is his wife.
Ox-King is his father-in-law.

Goku's birth name is: C) Kakarot

In one version of the future, Goku dies from a disease. HEART VIRUS

Who am I? TRUNKS

Spirit Bomb
Kamehameha Wave
Power Pole
Kaiokai Attack
Instant Transmission

PAGES 6–7 — VEGETA®

"To be the greatest Saiyan alive, like I always have been."

Unscramble these letters: NAPPA

Match each planet: 1-d, 2-c, 3-b, 4-a

How does Vegeta fit into the ruling family of his home planet? He is a prince.

Which is the highest level of warrior that Vegeta has achieved: C) Ascended Saiyan

During a battle with Goku, Vegeta did something in order to turn into an Oozaru: He created a moon.

Who am I? YARIJROBE

PAGES 8–9 — BUU™

Identify each of these Buu incarnations:

Kid _4_   Majin _1_   Super _3_   Evil _2_

Draw a line:

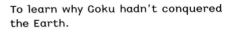

Unscramble these letters: MAJIN BUU

What character emerges that is actually all that is good in Buu? UUB

Who released Buu: B) BABIDI

Who am I? BIBIDI

When Buu was on a rampage: HERCULE

PAGES 10–11 — RADITZ™

To learn why Goku hadn't conquered the Earth.

At what level did Raditz come to Earth?
A) Saiyan

Unscramble these letters to find the name of the eyepiece Raditz wears: SCOUTER

Gives location of opponents
Acts as communicator
Gives power level of opponents

Who sacrificed himself to ensure the end of Raditz? GOKU

Who am I? CHIAOTZU

PAGES 12–13 — GOHAN®

Scorpions
Sabre-toothed tigers
Tyrannosaurs

One of Gohan's secret identities: GREAT SAIYAMAN

Who heals Gohan after he is injured battling Buu? B) Kibito

Gohan meets his future wife: VIDEL

Now unscramble these letters: HERCULE

Who am I? DABURA

One of Gohan's mighty feats: Legendary Z Sword

L Z R
E Y A
G N D

 Who am I? Oozaru

PAGES 14-15 — TRUNKS®

The names of the first two villains: King Cold and Cyborg Frieza

Trunks and Goten can fuse to form which character: A) Gotenks

In order for this fusion to take place, what must Trunks do with his power? Lower it.

 A future controlled by androids.

The names of Trunks's parents: Vegeta and Bulma

A M L
G T U
V E B

Who am I? Vegeta

PAGES 16-17 — GOTEN®

Raditz is his uncle, *Ox-King* is his grandfather, and *Chi-chi* is his mother.

Solve this equation to find out how old Goten was when he entered his first tournament:

4 quadrants · 3 levels = 7 years old

Goten teamed up with Trunks: MIGHTY MASK

S K T
A Y H
M I G

 He can fly
He can turn Super Saiyan without training
He is pure of heart

Draw a line: 30

A B C D

1
2
3

 A lesson from Hercule.

Who am I? OOLONG

PAGES 18-19 — DR. GERO™

Which Android was really Dr. Gero in disguise? C) 20

To find the location of Dr. Gero's hidden laboratory: In a cave outside North City.

Emergency Suspension Controller

Which of these androids did Dr. Gero not want activated? A) 16

Who am I? KIBITO

PAGES 20-21 — ANDROIDS™

Unscramble these letters: YAMCHA

Match each Android:
Absorbs energy — 19
Has incomplete programming — 16
Bluffed into retreat by Vegeta — 20
Manages to beat Vegeta — 18
Brother to another Android — 17

Who convinced Android 18 to forfeit the World Martial Arts Tournament? C) Hercule

The name of the inventor: Dr. Gero

The evil villain Cell set out to absorb: 17 and 18.

Who am I? PUI PUI

PAGES 22-23 — CELL®

Imperfect   Perfect   Junior

What does Cell have in common with Androids 17 and 18? All were created by Dr. Gero.

Piccolo
Vegeta
Frieza
Goku

One of the benefits of Cell's scorpion tail: Absorbs energy.

Which of these is not one of Cell's powers? C) Fire Breath

Unscramble these letters to find the name of the hero who finally defeated Cell: GOHAN

Cell received a great power from Goku's DNA: Instant Transmission

Who am I? TIEN

PAGES 24–25 — KING KAI™

Circle King Kai in this group of Kais.

Match each of the four quadrants of the universe with what it is best known for: 1-c, 2-d, 3-a, 4-b

Put these Kais in order: Supreme Kai, Grand Kai, King Kai

Decipher this message to find the names of King Kai's two companions: Gregory the Grasshopper and Bubbles the monkey

To find the name of the original rulers of the Kais: Daikaioh.

	1	2	3
1	A	D	H
2	I	K	O

Who am I? PIKKON

PAGES 26–27 — BULMA™

The name of one of Bulma's inventions: Dragon Radar.

Bulma has connections to many Dragon Ball Z characters.

Trunks is Bulma's son.

Great Saiyaman's costume was designed by Bulma.

Krillin
Gohan
Namek

Bulma is a technical genius who helped rebuild what character? Android 16

What is Bulma's most distinct personality trait? B) She can't stop talking.

Who am I? CAPTAIN GINYU

PAGES 28–29 — PAN™

Vibrant
Spunky
Fearless

Who are Pan's parents? C) Gohan and Videl

Find the path that will lead Pan to her favorite treat.

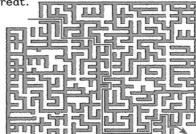

World Martial Arts Tournament

Who am I? KAMI

PAGES 30–31 — PICCOLO®

Can regenerate limbs
Energy blasts
Super speed
Beam cannon
Final flash
Can clone himself

Unscramble these letters: SUPER NAMEK

How did Piccolo come into being?
He's actually evil side of Kami.

Piccolo merged with this character to battle
Frieza: C) Nail

Who am I? EVIL BUU

PAGES 32–33 — MASTER ROSHI®

Master Roshi is known by two other names:
Turtle Hermit and Hermit Turtle

How did Master Roshi get these nicknames?
He lived on a deserted island with only a
turtle for companionship.

First earthling to nurture and control the
power of light.

Which pair of students studied under Master
Roshi? A) Goku & Krillin

The name of an attack that Master Roshi
taught both students: Kamehameha Wave

Who am I? GOHAN

PAGES 34–35 — KRILLIN®

Krillin's power was awakend by Guru. What
other character's power was also awakened
by Guru: Gohan

Krillin studied with Goku to become a great
fighter. The name of their teacher:
Master Roshi

Marries an android
Maron is his daughter
He's an earthling

Unscramble these letters: SENZU BEANS

What is Krillin's most powerful attack?
A) Destructo Disk

Who am I? ELDER KAI

PAGES 36–37 — FRIEZA®

He's the most powerful and evil being in
the universe.

The names of Frieza's two henchmen:
Dodoria and Zarbon

Frieza used a group of fighters to hold the
Dragon Balls on Namek: Ginyu Force

In a space pod
Large with horns
Largest with bent back
Smaller perfect form
Cyborg

Who gave Frieza the material for his cyborg
form? King Cold

Who am I? SHENRON

PAGES 38–39 — GARLIC JR.™

Which area is Garlic, Jr's specialty?
B) Mental Powers

Unscramble these letters to reveal the name
of the character: SHENRON

Mustard
Spice
Salt
Vinegar
The Spice Boys

Garlic Jr. came to Earth from somewhere in space: MAKYO STAR

After becoming immortal, Garlic Jr. was banished from the Earth: Dead Zone

```
QZD
NEA
 ↓
```

Only one thing can free a person from Garlic Jr's control: Sacred Water

```
      R
      W
      C
EDASRA
      E
      T
```

Who am I? KIBITOSHIN

PAGES 40–41 — DENDE™

Bring Piccolo back to life
Return Goku's energy
Bring Earthlings back to life

Who did Dende replace as guardian of the Earth? B) Kami

The names of the two people Dende lives:
Piccolo and Mr. Popo

What is Dende's main power? Healing

How many wishes do his Dragon Balls grant? Two

Who am I? VEGITO

PAGES 42–43 — SAIYANS™

GOKU
GOHAN
GOTEN
VEGETA
TRUNKS
GOTENKS

Which of these characters never received a Saiyan ranking? B) PICCOLO

Now match each fighter with an image.

VEGETA   GOTEN   TRUNKS

GOKU   GOHAN   GOTENKS

Who am I? TRUNKS